"I Never Knew You"

"To Whom Belongs the Glory"

Moreno Dal Bello

"...I NEVER KNEW YOU..."

Most professing Christians believe that there are two kinds of people: the saved and the unsaved, or, the believer and the unbeliever. There are no in-betweens and there are no gray areas. The Bible says, **"He that hath the Son hath life; and he that hath not the Son of God hath not life"** (1 Jn. 5:12). While it is true and correct to believe this, the Bible actually speaks of three types of people: the saved, made up of all true believers in God's one true Gospel; and those who are not saved, who do not believe the Gospel of Christ's Righteousness, this latter group is comprised of two sections, one of which is made up of those who ended their lives not believing in anything about God or Jesus Christ His Son, and the other, the third of our groups, or sub-group if you like, is made up of a multitude of religious people who were firmly convinced in their minds that they were Christians, that they *did* believe in God and yet the various gospels they held to were false gospels, evidencing the fact that they were all false christians!

So, we have those who believe, those who do not believe and those who believe they believe but believe amiss! This article will look at just who these people are who consider themselves believers but who are in reality unbelievers and what the Lord Jesus Christ will say to them on that Last Day.

The Gospel of Matthew is where we find the Lord Jesus addressing the three types of persons who inhabit the earth. What Christ will say to these three groups is seen in His teaching about the goats and the sheep. In Matthew 25:34, after describing His own people as **"sheep"**—those whom God has chosen from before the foundation of the world (Eph. 1:4); not according to their works but according to His own purpose and grace (2 Tim. 1:9); whom He had ordained (predestined) to believe in Him and who, in time, would do so (Acts 13:48); whom He had given, and therefore would come, to Jesus His Son (Jn. 6:37); for whom Christ died on the cross (Jn. 10:15) in order to pay for their sins (Isa. 53:8,11) to cancel the debt which they owed to God for their sins (Acts 13:39) thereby satisfying forever the wrath of God, having successfully delivered His people from that wrath (1 Thess. 1:10), and having washed away their sins and guilt (Col. 2:13,14 & Heb. 9:12,14), having their sins imputed to Him and His righteousness imputed to them (2 Cor. 5:21)—the Lord Jesus says to them, **"...Come ye blessed of My Father, inherit the Kingdom prepared for you from the foundation of the world"** (Matt. 25:34). Every true believer born of God, born of His Gospel, can expect to hear these blessed words from their Savior. What a glorious eternity awaits those who believe on Him as He is revealed in God's **power unto salvation:** the Mighty Gospel! What a marvellous and eternal bliss awaits those whose sins have been blotted out by the blood of Christ.

How wonderful is the everlasting love and mercy of the great and gracious God for His people.

Later, in the same passage of Scripture found in Matthew 25, we see the future unveiled, the ultimate and everlasting end, of all unbelievers. These unbelievers include all those who had no belief whatsoever in God and also those who professed to believe in Him, yet in reality did not. All such people are referred to as **"goats"** by the Lord Jesus and are eternally separated from God's sheep: **"And before Him shall be gathered all nations: and He shall separate them one from another, as a shepherd divideth his sheep from the goats: and He shall set the sheep on His right hand, but the goats on the left"** (Matt. 25:32,33). The goats have no part with the sheep. Their end is quite different from that of the sheep, but just as certain and just as real. Jesus the Lord and Judge over all mankind says to these goats in Matthew 25:41: **"...Depart from Me, ye cursed, into everlasting fire, prepared for the Devil and his angels."** Eternal torment awaits those who die in their sins; who enter into eternity with their sins unforgiven. They will spend eternity in endless and intolerable agony and **"...the smoke of their torment ascendeth up for ever and ever..."** (Rev. 14:11). Their eternal suffering and unbearable torment is due to the fact that they died unrepentant sinners who took pleasure in their rebellion against God.

Now to the third group: the ones who were convinced they were Christians but never were;

the ones who were convinced they believed in the Truth but were deceived by a lie which they trusted in and embraced; the ones who took just as much pleasure in, and yet were quite ignorant of, their rebellion against the true God and their real spiritual condition before Him. This group of religiously minded people who come from the four corners of religion, from the Roman Catholic world, the Pentecostal/Charismatic world, the Arminian world and the Cultic world will go to the same end, for they are all part of the second group mentioned earlier: **the goats.** Their destiny is also an everlasting fire that torments and which does not cease day or night. But there is something different about these goats. You see, though they too are goats well and true and always had been, they *believed* themselves to be sheep. As far as they were concerned, and according to what they had been taught, they did not live or die rejecting Christ but proclaimed His name to the very end. In fact, many of them were convinced that they'd even prophesied in His name, and also cast out devils in His name. Most claimed they'd performed, to their minds at least, many wonderful works in His name (see Matt. 7:22) and that God had given them grace to enable them to repent of much immorality and illicit conduct. These people, and there will be a multitude on that final day, also called Jesus *"Lord"* and therefore believed Him to be God and worshipped Him as such. They all prayed and worshipped. Many of them lived exemplary lives seeking to help, and being mindful of, others and careful not to disobey God's Law but to live as good a life as they possibly could. As far as these people were concerned, all the evidence around them was enough to convince them they were Christians: they 'believed', they read their Bibles, they had been baptised, they treated their fellow man fairly and lovingly, they attended 'church' every week and sang their hymns and choruses with great gusto and read all the respected 'christian' authors etc., etc., yet despite all their religiosity and piety, these people will receive the most chilling, the most terrifying and most shocking pronouncements of all. God the Son, Jesus Christ, the one whom they all believed they loved and followed, will look upon them without mercy and without love and profess unto them, **"...I NEVER KNEW YOU: depart from Me, ye that work iniquity"** (Matt. 7:23). You will notice that the words **"depart from Me"** are the exact same words the Lord Jesus says to all the accursed goats in Matthew 25. Jesus also said, **"Many will say to Me in that day, 'Lord, Lord'..."** (Matt. 7:22), yet they were among the deceived and deluded ones; they worshipped Him in vain; they were goats and not sheep and their faith was as worthless as that of demons (Jas. 2:19). Their names had NEVER been written in the Lamb's Book of Life from the foundation of the world (Rev. 17:8; 20:15), unlike those of the elect. The Lord **"...knoweth them that trust in Him"** (Nah. 1:7) but not those who trust in false gods. These whom the God of Grace had never known and who therefore had never truly known the Grace of God, had never at any stage of their lives been Christians. **They had either believed they were, or that others could be, saved before or without hearing and believing the Gospel of Christ.** They had never once been born again, born of the Gospel of God, and preserved in Christ, though for all appearances many, including themselves, believed they had been, and were, Christians. These accursed ones, as the Lord calls them, were not those whom many believe had at one time professed belief in Christ and later abandoned Him, for their names had NEVER been written in the Lamb's Book of Life from the foundation of the world (Rev. 17:8). **Jesus did not say to them, "I ONCE knew you but not any longer."** Christ declares that He NEVER knew them, He never had a covenant relationship with any of them, He NEVER knew them in the intimate and personal way He knows His sheep, those who are His own. **He NEVER knew them as His sheep but only ever recognized them as goats and therefore they were NEVER saved!** Also, the Lord Jesus states that the true sheep, His sheep, shall **NEVER** perish! (Jn. 10:28,29). They are eternally contrasted with those whom Christ Jesus says He *does* know: *"My sheep hear My voice, and I KNOW THEM, and they follow Me"* (Jn. 10:27,28), and *"I am the good shepherd, and know My sheep, and am known of Mine"* (Jn. 10:14). Scripture says *"...the Lord knoweth them that are His..."* (2 Tim. 2:19). It stands to biblical reason therefore that if the Lord does not know you then it is clear that you are not, never have been and never will be, His. He never loved the goats but only His Church, the sheep, for whom He gave up His life. Jesus said: **"...I lay down My life for the sheep"** (Jn. 10:15; cf. Eph. 5:25). Those whom the Lord does not know were not *once* saved and then fell away and lost their salvation. How could this be, for they were NEVER saved in the first place! **Christ had never laid down His life for them.** To have been saved they must have at one time been sheep and therefore their names must at least temporarily have been written in the Lamb's Book of Life—pencilled in only to later be rubbed out. **But Scripture states emphatically that their names were NEVER at any time written in the Lamb's Book of Life, hence they could never have been sheep.** These are all people who called Him *"Lord"* to the very end of their lives and are among those Jesus referred to when He said: **"Not every one that saith unto Me, Lord, Lord, shall enter into the Kingdom of heaven..."** (Matt. 7:21). **At no stage had Jesus the Christ ever called these people His and therefore at no time could He have been the one they had trusted in.** They were not among the elect, the chosen ones of God. They had never been ordained to eternal life. The Lord Jesus did not die for their sins; He did not lay down His life for the goats; He did not plant the tares; He did not die for the tares for they were of their father the Devil (Matt. 13:38,39). He NEVER knew them and they NEVER knew Him. **They are such an accursed lot that they all share in the**

very fate of the Devil and his angels! They are part of the Devil's herd, not God's flock! They all died in their sins with a religion of their own making, a jesus of their own imagination and a vain belief in doctrinal error, which is always indicative of a false gospel, which cannot save. These who professed to be Christians yet who believed in a christ that was espoused to them out of a false gospel, which is by definition NOT the power of God unto salvation, these people who called Him *"Lord"* and yet were never known by Him, and who therefore worshipped Him in vain, are among those described for us in 2 Thessalonians 2:10 who *"...**perish; because they received not the love of the truth that they might be saved.**"* One must have a love of the truth and therefore a saving belief in that truth, as revealed in the Gospel, to be saved. These people were not given justifying faith but were sent strong delusion by God **"...THAT they should believe a lie: THAT they all might be damned who believed not the truth but had pleasure in unrighteousness"** (2 Thess. 2:11,12). Though there was obviously a head-knowledge, an intellectual acknowledgment to some of the truths of God, these workers of iniquity only possessed a form of godliness but always denied the power thereof (2 Tim. 3:5), **"Ever learning, and never able to come to the knowledge of the truth"** (2 Tim. 3:7). They were not, and could not possibly have ever been, of God for Jesus Himself tells them, ***"I NEVER knew you..."*** **Christ never knew them as what**

they believed and professed themselves to be—Christians and therefore His people. He only and always knew them as accursed goats whom He would one day command to depart from His presence.

Specifically, who are these people? It is clear from their addressing Christ Jesus as *"Lord"* that they cannot be J.W.'s, or Hindus, or Buddhists, or Muslims or any other group who deny the Lordship and therefore the Deity of Jesus Christ. These goats called Him *"Lord"*, obviously believing Him to be Lord and God, yet He did not know them—NOT EVER!! **They believed in a jesus but not THE Jesus; they believed in a gospel but not THE Gospel; they were guided by a spirit but it was not THE Holy Spirit of God.** Such things are possible, in fact they happen every day. People being deceived by fraudulent gospels into believing they have the true God when all they have is a false god, an impotent counterfeit who cannot save. Incidentally, not every false god goes by the name of Allah or Buddha. The worst and most deceptive of false gods are called 'god' and 'jesus'. **The right names and titles of God are often used in false gospels which promote false gods that can only provide people with a false sense of security.** One might feel safe in calling one's god 'jesus' but is it the Jesus which the true God reveals in His Gospel?

It is important to note that Christ does not <u>disown</u> these people, but by His words recorded for us in Matthew 7 it is quite

evident that **He had never owned them to begin with.** They were NEVER His for He NEVER *once* called them His *brethren,* or even *former brethren,* they had never fallen away from Him for they had never truly come to Him! They were NEVER drawn to Him by the Father (Jn. 6:44). **There NEVER was a work of God performed in them and, as evidenced by their belief of a false Gospel, had never been given saving faith to believe God's one and only Gospel.** They were NEVER blessed of God; Jesus Christ did not bare their sins on the cross and therefore they were never at any stage of their lives made acceptable unto the Father, for their sins remained unatoned for and they were clothed only with a righteousness of their own. **They were never in Christ and so were never of Christ.** If this were not the case, then it must be asked for what purpose would Jesus Christ have died for the sins of those whose names had never been written in the Lamb's Book of Life from before the foundation of the world, those whom God had not ordained to eternal life?

Returning to the question *Who are these people?* most may be found within, but not exclusive to, the Charismatic movement, the Pentecostal movement, the Faith movement, the Roman Catholic Church, all Arminian assemblies as well as the Seventh-Day Adventist churches. They are also found in Calvinist groups, where most believe that Arminians are saved regardless of the false gospel they believe. **NOT ALL** the people in these movements are amongst those whom Jesus NEVER knew, for God has and will continue to bring out all His own from these organizations; from believing in false gospels into His marvellous Light where is revealed His one and only Gospel. (Lk. 15:4-6). But **most** of the people in the above named groups *will* be found among those to whom the Lord Jesus will one day formally utter those dreaded words, **"I NEVER KNEW YOU: Depart from Me, ye that work iniquity!"** Every Charismatic, Faith movement follower, Roman Catholic, Seventh-Day Adventist and believer in every form of Arminianism and every tolerant Calvinist believes that Jesus is Lord and refers to Him as such. And, as the Scriptures say, many will claim to have prophesied and cast out devils in His name and done many good and wonderful works in His name, and yet there NEVER was a work of regeneration by the Holy Spirit performed in them. **The principal evidence for this lies in the fact that they never turned from their false gospels and were never led by God's Spirit of Truth to the true Gospel of God, the one which says:** man is dead in sin and cannot come to God in and of himself (Matt. 19:25,26; Rom. 3:10,11; Eph. 2:1,12); that God chose a people for Himself before the foundation of the world, not based on anything they did but upon His will, wisdom and grace and according to His purpose (Eph. 1:3-6; 2 Tim. 1:9); that Christ Jesus was sent to the earth to establish a perfect righteousness, to die for these people God had chosen and entrusted to Christ's care (Jn. 10:27,28; 17:2,3; Eph. 5:25);

that their sins would be charged to Him and His Righteousness to them, thus making them wholly acceptable unto God (2 Cor. 5:21; Eph. 5:2); that all these people would believe His Gospel and be saved, for this is the will of God and none of them will perish (Jn. 10:26-29). The one thing that stands out like a sore thumb about all these people is they believed in a gospel which God was not the author of. Whilst calling Jesus *"Lord"*, these goats who believed they were sheep believed many untruths about Him, thereby actually placing their trust in *another jesus* a savior of their own making, a jesus of their own imagination. They denied the sufficiency of His precious blood alone shed upon the cross as a full and complete atonement for the sins of His people. They added to His death false teachings necessary, they claimed, to secure salvation. In their adding to His death they actually take away from His glorious work. They, therefore, preach *another* gospel about *another* christ and are filled with *another* spirit and not that Holy Spirit of God Who leads and guides all the elect, all the sheep, into Truth.

      The apostle Paul's response to the Jewish believers' desire that circumcision be included in the Gospel of Christ, thereby perverting and making it a denial of Christ rather than a promoter and revealer of Him, is clear. In Galatians 1:8 Paul says, **"But though we, or an angel from heaven, preach any other gospel unto you than that which we have preached unto you, LET HIM BE ACCURSED."** Something as small and as seemingly insignificant as the cutting away of the foreskin of a male, when added to the Gospel of Christ, was significant enough to pervert it entirely, thereby producing a false gospel which, if any man preached or believed, would render and demonstrate that one to be in an accursed state. The Bible says that **"A little leaven leaveneth the whole lump"** (Gal. 5:9). If such a seemingly insignificant thing as adding circumcision to the cross renders a man accursed, how much more so when he directly takes away or adds to the finished work of Christ on the Tree? Only belief in the true Gospel of God is the gateway to Heaven and all His sheep have/will believe it. Only **"...the TRUTH shall make you free"** (Jn. 8:32). Those who do not believe God's Gospel, either by not believing anything about God or by falling for the lies contained in false gospels, reveal themselves as goats and shall be judged accordingly. Remember, **"...the Lord Jesus shall be revealed from heaven with His mighty angels, in flaming fire taking vengeance on them that know not God, and that obey not the Gospel of our Lord Jesus Christ"** (2 Thess. 1:7,8).

"TO WHOM BELONGS THE GLORY?"

Q. How much glory for salvation belongs to God?

Doubtless there are few, if any, who lay claim to being Christian that would answer this question with any other word than ALL. God is deserving of all the glory for salvation. When it comes to the matter of how much glory, how much praise, God is worthy of in the salvation of a human being, all who claim to be Christian should have no hesitation in saying that God deserves all the glory. **He deserves all the praise for the salvation of a person because He has done everything necessary to save a man AND keep him saved.** Be they 'Calvinist' or 'Arminian,' true believers in God's Gospel or all who profess to believe, none would dare say that God is not deserving of all the glory for every bit of salvation.

Q. Why?

Why does God alone deserve all the glory? Why should all the praise for salvation belong to God alone? Why is it not partly shared with man? The Arminian who asserts that man plays an active part in his own salvation by choosing to come to God out of his own free will claims to believe that God alone is worthy of all praise and glory for salvation. But how can he justify his when he also says that without man making a decision to come to God, God would be without any saved souls and His Kingdom would be without a people. Many Arminians try and counter this by saying that they do give God all the glory, for they say that without His grace present none could choose Him. They fail to realise that any act on man's behalf, anything motivated by his own so-called 'free will', constitutes a meritable act, something that deserves praise and to which God is obliged to respond. **If you condition any part of salvation on man, then once he has complied with that condition he must surely be deserving of some glory.** After all, the Arminian claims that man's 'decision' is that which makes the difference between him and the one who chooses not to come to God. Such people place themselves in the same category as the Pharisee in Luke 18 who praised God for what *he* was like and what *he* did but whom Jesus referred to as one who exalted *himself* and not God—he went home an unjustified man, still in his sins (see Lk. 18:9-14).

The true Christian knows who it is that makes him to differ from the lost man: ***"For who maketh thee to differ from another? And what hast thou that thou didst not receive? Now if thou didst receive it, why dost thou glory, as if thou hadst not received it?"*** (1 Cor. 4:7). Everything a believer is and everything a believer has is given to him. In other words the salvation of man, the fact that he is now a new creature in Christ, is due to God having given to man that which man could not choose or come to of his own accord.

Q. If God deserves all the glory for every detail in the salvation of a man, what does this make the man?

From start to finish God did everything necessary to save those whom He elected before the world began. **God did all the work, so then to Him alone belongs all the glory.** Every detail, right down to causing a man to come to Him, was prepared and fulfilled by God. *"Blessed is the man whom Thou choosest, and causest to approach unto Thee..."* (Psa. 65:4). No man can come to God of his own volition or his own power: *"Thy people shall be willing in the day of THY power..."* (Psa. 110:3). God chooses man. God is the cause, or catalyst, behind a man coming to Him and only in the day of God's power shall a man be willing to come to Him. The Lord Jesus said, *"No man CAN come to Me, except the Father which hath sent Me draw him..."* (Jn. 6:44). Man does not choose to come to God, man is drawn by God. A man does not *find God* but is found of God. The following Scripture specifies in detail what exactly God has done in saving a man and at the same time it reveals man to be a mere recipient of that which is a result of the love of God, found only in Christ His Son: *"...whom HE did predestinate, them HE also called: and whom HE called, them HE also justified: and whom HE justified, them HE also glorified"*

(Rom. 8:30). There is no room for man here; no requirement or condition he must meet; nothing he can do to get himself saved or keep himself saved and therefore no reason for any glory to be attributed to man in his own salvation. **God gets all the glory because He has done all the work!!** God elected, God predestined, God prepared the substitutionary sacrifice and His Son became that sacrifice which would wash away every sin of those people God entrusted to Him, and which would satisfy the justice of God and forever put an end to the wrath of God towards those people and their sins. It is by **GOD'S WILL** that any are saved: ***"...them that believe on His name: which were born, not of blood, nor of the will of the flesh, nor of the will of man, but of God"*** (Jn. 1:12,13); ***"So then it*** (salvation) ***is not of him that willeth, nor of him that runneth, but of God that sheweth mercy"*** (Rom. 9:16). Salvation is something that is all up to God. It is something for Him to bestow, not for us to attain. ***"Not by works of righteousness which we have done, but according to His mercy He saved us..."*** (Titus 3:5). Salvation does not take the will or work of man but the mercy of God! ***"Of HIS OWN WILL begat He us with the Word of truth..."*** (Jas. 1:18). Man's 'will' always comes in second to God's will. **If a man 'wills' to come to God and be saved, it is of a surety that God first willed the man to be saved, then made the man willing.** A man is not saved because he believes, but he believes because he is saved. God's Son took the sins of His Father's chosen upon Himself and charged those people with His perfect Righteousness (2 Cor. 5:21). By His mercy God drew those people to Him. All who are saved love God but only because He loved them first (1 Jn. 4:19). **First the Savior then salvation.** Yes they received Him but only *after* He had come to them, making them alive unto Him and granting them the gift of faith, the gift to believe that can only come from above and without which no man can savingly believe His Gospel and reject all others. God loved the *ungodly*, those who were His enemies, those who did not know Him or seek Him (Rom. 5:6,8). **God did it all.** Salvation is all of God. Salvation is all of grace. It is a gift that none can merit. If it could be something earned it would not be a gift and salvation would not be by grace. And if salvation were not by grace, then it would at least partly be by works and so God would then not be entitled to all the glory for salvation but would have to share that glory with man. **"...*if it be of works, then is it no more grace...*"** (Rom. 11:6). The Scriptures tell us that salvation is "...***of faith, that it might be by grace...***" and not a work of man's, not by anything he has done or can do. **Justification by faith rules out any possibility of any part of salvation being conditioned on man** (see Gal. 3:24 & Eph. 2:8,9). The faith that saves comes from God and is granted at His discretion. Salvation is not by works. Therefore no part of it could be conditioned on man. **Salvation is BY GRACE THROUGH FAITH, it is not of man, in other words, no**

part of it is conditioned on man. It is a gift from God and no part of it is a result of the efforts of man. Why? SO THAT NO MAN CAN BOAST!! So that no man could ever rightly claim any glory for any part of salvation. **And if no man can ever rightly lay claim to any of the glory for salvation, it would be an insane act to subscribe to the abominable lie that any part of salvation is conditioned, reliant, on man.** Faith goes hand in hand with grace and is the antithesis of works. Salvation cannot be by grace *and* works for the one nullifies the other. Salvation is not by grace *and* works but a case of *either* grace *or* works. It is all of grace or all of works (see Gal. 3:10; 5:3). Paul the apostle said, **"I do not frustrate the grace of God: for if righteousness come by the law, then Christ is dead in vain"** (Gal. 2:21). Salvation by faith points to grace not works. It points to what God has done not what we have to do. And grace points to God and He alone is deserving of all the glory for salvation. The faith spoken of here is the faith of Christ that justifies a man: **"...a man is not justified by the works of the law, but by the faith of Jesus Christ..."** (Gal. 2:16). That is, a man is justified by true faith in Christ which comes only from Christ. **So then, if salvation is by grace then it is ALL of grace, it is a work of God so it stands to reason it is ALL of God and therefore ALL the glory for it belongs to Him.** No supplementary act by man is required to either save him or keep him saved. It is **"...by the OBEDIENCE OF ONE..."** (Rom. 5:19) that a person is made righteous and remains in a state of righteousness before God. If no glory for salvation belongs to man, then it is logical and right to believe that man plays no part in his own salvation. It is a gift from God and a gift is bestowed not earned. Now, this does not mean that a saved man does not need to be obedient etc., it means that his salvation does not depend on his obedience but only upon that obedience of Christ. **Christ got him saved and it is Christ Who keeps him saved.**

Q. So what is man; what is his role in salvation?

The answer is quite simple: man is a recipient! He is a vessel of God's mercy. He plays no part in his salvation for no part of salvation is conditioned on man. **Humanly speaking he must believe but this believing is an evidence of his salvation rather than the cause of it.** It is an evidence of God having come to the man and revealing His Mighty Gospel to him, providing the faith necessary to believe it. Nothing a man does can get himself saved, keep himself saved or effect the loss of his salvation. **All are dead in sin before God comes to a man and what can a dead man do? NOTHING!** According to natural man's thinking, which is the foundation of all false religion, there can be no salvation without man's compliance, without his 'decision' to accept what is 'put on offer' to him. **How, though, can a man comply, how can a man accept what is 'on**

offer' if every man in his natural fallen state is dead to God, does not seek Him and therefore could never want Him? God must initiate and so therefore if God must be the one to make the first move before a man can approach Him, if God is the cause, the initiator, the author of it all then to God belongs all the glory, for without Him man would be forever dead, forever lost. Nothing man does, even his believing, can be attributed to him as worthy of praise and be counted as something he has done to complete God's plan of salvation for him. Man is saved not because of anything he has done. **Salvation is not because of man, it is because of God.** You will also find God behind every good work a saved person does: *"For we are His workmanship, created in Christ Jesus unto good works, which God hath before ordained that we should walk in them"* (Eph. 2:10). A person is saved as a result of *"...the purpose of God according to election, not of works, but of Him that calleth"* (Rom. 9:11). *"(God) hath saved us, and called us with an holy calling, not according to our works, but according to His own purpose and grace, which was given us in Christ Jesus before the world began"* (2 Tim. 1:9). Salvation was sorted and settled even before the world began, so how could any boast in what they had done, with or without the grace of God, to 'get themselves saved.' Man's believing, just as with his repentance, is a gift from God. It is not something that comes from within but is a gift given from without. Without God no man would ever believe, so it is easy to see that to God belongs all the glory. The Christian is not found in Christ because of any condition he has fulfilled but the Scripture says: **"...OF HIM are ye in Christ Jesus..."** (1 Cor. 1:30). **Salvation is by grace through faith because it is a work of God's and not man's.** All of salvation is because of God. None of it is conditioned on man because no man could ever even begin to fulfill any condition to become saved. How, for instance, would a man believe or even want to believe the true God when there is nothing in him that prompts him to even seek God! **And what could a man do to keep himself saved? If his salvation demanded perfection, could his salvation be maintained by anything less?** Of course not. All of salvation is because of God's unmerited love for His chosen ones and not the smallest degree of glory or praise is deserved by man for he is a mere recipient, a receptacle of God's love and grace and mercy, deserving of nothing yet given everything. Man is saved because of the love of God and he remains saved because of the love of God in Christ. **Salvation is all about God not man.** Salvation is all about the glory of God not the glory of man. Salvation is all about what God has done and the true Christian boasts not in himself, his language is not *'See what God has enabled me to do'* or *'I chose God,'* but rather **"Come and hear, all ye that fear God, and I will declare what HE HATH DONE for my soul"** (Psa. 66:16). A man God has chosen does not approach God saying *"I choose you"* but rather **"...God be merciful to** *me a sinner"* (Lk. 18:13). The Christian is not the one who chooses God but it is God Who chooses him. **THAT IS THE UNDERLYING PRINCIPAL OF GRACE!!** Rather than 'boasting' in their 'choice of God', the Christian praises God for making him a part of His chosen generation. Christians are not a generation of choosers but *"...a chosen generation...* (1 Pet. 2:9). True believers do not rejoice in a newly converted person having 'chosen God' but because God from the beginning has chosen them to be saved (see 2 Thess. 2:13). Salvation is all about the beauty of God not the 'goodness' of man. Salvation is about the grace of God, in other words, it is about what God has done. **Salvation is not about what man has to do but what the Lord has done.** Salvation, glory, praise, grace, mercy and faith are things which come from God and so are designed to point people to Him, that we might look upon Him and see the glory of His Nature and fill our hearts with praise for Him, the only one deserving of any glory or praise for salvation. No one looks to themselves in adoration after they have been given a gift but are thankful and praise-filled towards the gift giver. They rave about the gift giver and what he has done and not about themselves, for they have nothing to boast about in themselves that they have acquired a gift. **When contemplating the gift, one cannot but think about the one who has given the gift.** We do not consider ourselves as having earned the gift but rather our boasting and our thanks are towards the gift giver for his generosity and kindness. **We are mere**

recipients who do not deserve praise but are obliged to praise the gift giver, for without him we would have nothing.

By nature man is dead in sin but God is alive. **Man did not seek God but it is God Who sought and found him** (see Rom. 3:11 & Lk. 15:4,5 & Ezek. 34:11,12). **Man is a sinner, God is the Savior.** Man did not believe, God gave him the faith to believe. Before God made him alive man was dead, spiritually stagnant and stuck in a miry pit of his own making. **A nowhere man with nowhere to go and no way of getting there.** Before God loved the man, the man did not love God. Before a man was saved he was lost. Before man had hope he was hopeless. Before he was given the faith to believe God's Gospel man at best believed a false gospel. No man can come to God, no man has ever come to Him on his own accord. Nothing within a man can prompt him to seek the true God. Unless God has drawn the man he remains in his lost, spiritually debauched state, a hopeless creature. Without God there is no hope (Eph. 2:12). Man has nothing he can turn to, not within him or without him, that can get him saved for without God man is hope-less. The Lord Jesus said that with man salvation was an utter impossibility (see Matt. 19:26). But with God all things are possible, yes, even the salvation of a man **but it takes God to make it happen.** It is not a case of man coming to God and saying, *'Save me for I cannot'*. How dare any man, in his spiritually dead state, presume that he can approach God anyway! **"...*every man at his*

best state is altogether vanity" (Psa. 39:5). No man can come to God or even wants the true God before God comes to the man first. **Nothing man can do inspires God to save him. Man cannot make the fist move or any move towards God before God comes to the man first. As long as salvation is all of grace all the glory for it will belong to God.** With God there is hope! With God a man can be saved! So, if man on his own is without hope, how can he possibly attain to salvation? If man could do something to prompt God to save him then he would not be without hope. The roles would be reversed and it would be God Who would have no hope unless man consented to receive Him, unless man came to God first. Scripture makes it perfectly clear: **"There is none that understandeth, there is none that seeketh after God"** (Rom. 3:11). How could man ever be responsible for any part of salvation if he is a creature so plagued with sin, so devastated by his sinful nature, he cannot know God and therefore does not even seek God? It is important to note that God is not to blame for man's spiritually dead state, but it is man alone who must take the blame and reap the consequences if God is not merciful to him. **How can any man choose that which he does not seek?** And in light of this, how could any man seriously claim that he ever chose God? **There is no salvation without God therefore all the glory for salvation must belong to God.** Salvation is conditioned on the will of God not the will of man. God has done it all and any gospel that conditions any part of salvation on what a man must do is a gospel that does not give all the glory for salvation to God, but is a perverted message designed to exalt man. It is a message which has not come from God but from the imagination of man. **Anyone believing they were saved when they adhered to a gospel that conditioned salvation, to any degree, on themselves, regardless of what they now claim to believe, is as lost as they can be.**

To God be the glory, great things HE has done. We praise God, not for that which He has enabled us to do but for that which HE has done. The emphasis, the focus, is all on Him for He makes the saved man to differ from the lost. He is the Savior, He is the Light, He is the Hope, He is the Provider and He is the Justifier. God justifies a man by imputing to him the very Righteousness of His Son Jesus Christ (see Rom. 4:6). A man is saved by Christ's righteousness and a man can only remain saved by that righteousness. **So that which justifies us before God is of Him and not us therefore He rightly gets all the glory for salvation.** We praise God for what His Son has done that we could never do; for what His Son has done on behalf of His people. All the glory for salvation from beginning to end belongs to God and He shares this glory with no man.

I doubt whether there is any man who would dare teach that to man belongs even some of the glory for salvation. Even those who insist that the final decision for salvation belongs to man and without it he remains lost, would not claim any glory for themselves, in so many words, but in making God's plan of salvation ultimately hinge on a man's free will decision, or a man obeying in order to remain saved, everyone who adheres to these deadly errors in reality exalts themselves and not God (see the article 'The Pharisee and the Publican'). The moment you include the word 'I' when speaking about salvation you immediately shift the focus from God to yourself. Salvation is all about God and what He has done. **HIS** Love, **HIS** Grace, **HIS** Mercy, **HIS** Forgiveness, **HIS** Son, **HIS** Sacrifice, **HIS** Blood, **HIS** Obedience, **HIS** Death, **HIS** Righteousness. Just as with the beneficiary of a last will and testament, the truly saved man is an eternal beneficiary of God's Will for him and he is forever grateful and thankful to God and what He has done knowing that he, the man, has never and could never do anything to get himself saved or keep himself saved.

Salvation is all of God, therefore no part of it is conditioned on man and therefore no part of the glory for salvation can be rightly assigned to man, for there is nothing he can do in order to get himself saved or keep himself in a saved state. Yes, he must believe but this believing can only come when God grants His gift of faith, which exclusively believes and holds dear His one and only Gospel.

"But I am like a green olive tree in the house of God: I trust in the mercy of God for ever

and ever. I will praise Thee for ever, because Thou hast done it: and I will wait on Thy name; for it is good before Thy saints" (Psa. 52:8,9).

"I will greatly rejoice in the Lord, my soul shall be joyful in my God; for He hath clothed me with the garment of salvation, He hath covered me with the robe of righteousness..." (Isa. 61:10).

"But I have trusted in THY mercy; my heart shall rejoice in THY salvation" (Psa. 13:5).

THE FATAL ERROR OF BELIEVING A FALSE GOSPEL

The reason it is a fatal error not to believe the truth of Gospel essentials such as sovereign election by the free grace and will of God, the substitutionary atonement of Jesus Christ, the eternal security of the man whom God has elected unto salvation and for whom Christ has died, and that unless one is submitted to the Righteousness of Christ one cannot be saved, is that **not believing these truths, or even being undecided, shows that one is believing something other than the Truth of God which, naturally, would contradict His truth. That which does not come from God is that which opposes Him and what He has said. The person who believes in that which God has not said is in ignorance/darkness, which is what a person in a saved state is brought out from in the first place. Either way, they are not believing the Truth.**

Belief of the truth, which is revealed in the doctrine of God and in which every true believer abides (2 Jn. 9), is what distinguishes a saved person, who has been brought out of darkness into God's marvellous Light, from a person who is lost and sitting in darkness. The state of every man by nature is shown clearly in the following verse: *"Having the understanding darkened, being alienated from the life of God through the ignorance that is in them, because of the blindness of their heart"* (Eph. 4:18 cf. Jn. 1:5). **The blinded heart cannot pump the blood of eternal life. None are born again who remain in darkness and ignorance of what the Gospel is:** *"...if our Gospel be hid, it is hid to them that are lost"* (2 Cor. 4:3). If the Gospel is hid to any man, he cannot see it and he is therefore ignorant of it. This is evidence that he is lost, for God has not revealed His truth to Him. The truth of God is revealed to His elect, and to others it is not given: *"...it is given unto you to know the mysteries of the kingdom of heaven, but to them it is not given....he that received seed into the good ground is he that heareth the word, and understandeth it"* (Matt. 13:11,23). Just as in physical birth one is brought out of darkness (the womb), so too, in spiritual birth one is brought out of darkness (ignorance of the truth) into God's marvellous Light—His Truth. **Ignorance is an unmistakeable sign of lostness.** Ignorance is the womb, if you will, from which a man receives no sustenance but is brought out of when he is given birth to by God through His Truth (Jas. 1:18).

The Bible teaches that one cannot believe in the true Christ whilst in ignorance of Who He is and what He has done.**One is not born as long as one is in the womb—one is not born again as long as one is in ignorance.** Only**after** one has heard of the true Christ can one rightly claim to believe in Him: *"In Whom* (Christ) *ye also trusted, AFTER that ye heard the Word of*

Truth, THE GOSPEL of your salvation: in Whom also AFTER that ye believed, ye were sealed with that Holy Spirit of promise" (Eph. 1:13). This Scripture shows beyond a shadow of a doubt that one cannot believe in the true Christ **who has not had that Christ revealed to them** via the word of truth, His doctrine: His Gospel. The only hope for sinners is revealed in God's Gospel Message: ***"For the hope which is laid up for you in heaven, whereof ye heard before IN THE WORD OF THE TRUTH OF THE GOSPEL"*** (Col. 1:5). The message of the sure hope of Heaven lies in the doctrines of the Gospel and none can bear fruit unto God before **they hear His Gospel and know** the grace of God **IN TRUTH** (see Col. 1:6 cf. Matt. 13:23). One cannot believe and trust in Christ until *after* one has *heard* His Gospel and none are sealed with that Holy Spirit of promise who have not *believed* that glorious Gospel, wherein Christ and His Righteousness are revealed, and rejected **all** others (Rom. 1:16,17).

    One cannot have true saving God-given Faith if one does not believe the one, true, God-given Gospel. One cannot have true saving faith if one believes that one was saved whilst believing in another gospel, because true saving faith trusts only in one Gospel and believes only one Gospel to be the truth, and only one Gospel that can save. This would be like a person who wrongly imagined twelve inches to be a certain length, then upon discovering how long twelve inches really was, **nevertheless insisting that**

their previous appraisal was just as accurate as that deemed by the ruler! None are saved whilst insisting they were saved *before* hearing and 'believing' THE Gospel, for the very Gospel of God which such people claim to believe denies that such a thing is possible! Such people often base their salvation on a variety of experiences and see such life-changing and morally reforming episodes as unquestionable proof of spiritual rebirth, despite the absence of the Seed of God by which a man is born again: the Gospel! **God recognises only one Gospel as His and so do all His people.** The Gospel of God will have no part of a person who professes his love for it and yet is *married* to another gospel. Imagine getting married to a person who insists on bringing along their previous husband/wife!! **One must be dead to all other gospels before one can savingly and rightly be joined to God's Gospel. The Gospel of God cannot be yoked together with someone who believes they were saved prior to hearing and believing it and who will not reject every other gospel they previously believed in.** This would be like having two wives—a case of spiritual bigamy if you will. Equally, none are saved who insist that such a person is saved or who says a person that has not heard or does not believe THE Gospel is saved regardless. **For they are saying—contrary to what the Gospel declares—that one can be ignorant of the Gospel—wilfully or otherwise—and be nonetheless saved. Salvation, then, would be something based**

on a person's sincerity and 'genuine desire for God' rather than on God's genuine love for a person, shown by His revealing His Gospel to them and providing them with the faith to believe it. Any gospel that is not THE Gospel simply cannot save. *"He that believeth and is baptized shall be saved; but he that believeth not shall be damned"* (Mk. 16:16).

There is no contingency plan of salvation for those who believe error about Christ. There is no likelihood that any of God's chosen will not believe His Gospel in its entirety. One hireling informed this author that he does not know how much error God is willing to put up with in His people. The answer is: **no error that contributes to the perversion of the Gospel of Christ, thereby revealing another gospel that God has not declared and another christ that God does not claim to be HIS Son**, will be tolerated. Error is the spoiler. Error is the leaven that leaveneth the whole lump. **God never overlooks the error that leavens the whole lump** (see Gal 5:9). **Fatal error is that which changes truth into a lie and THE Gospel into <u>another</u> gospel.** No one has ever been saved by acknowledging error! **Heaven is for lovers of the truth, not those who are enamoured with a lie.** Those who believe a lie, ie. another gospel, far from being saved, are under strong delusion (2 Thess. 2:11). There are no allowances made in God's plan of salvation for those who believe error, for the whole idea of that

Great Plan is that it be believed in order that people be saved. **Knowledge of God's Truth is the fulfilment of God's Plan for the salvation of His people.**

Saving faith ALWAYS believes THE TRUE Gospel, never a false one, for it is the faith that comes from God (2 Thess. 2:13,14). The faith which does not save, which does not come from God as His gift, is that which believes salvation can either come before or without belief in God's only Gospel. **The Faith that God gives finds refuge, comfort and security ONLY in the doctrine of Christ. The faith that finds refuge, comfort and security in anything other than the doctrine of Christ ALONE hasn't come from God.**

The majority of this article was excerpted from the author's book 'Election Is Just Not Fair!' which may be viewed at www.godsonlygospel.com

This article is also available on request in the Philippino 'Tagalog' language.

Please Contact:

morenodalbello@yahoo.com.au

Please Visit:

www.godsonlygospel.com

Made in the USA
Monee, IL
03 May 2026

49437962R00022